Supporting Grammar and Language Development in Children

This guidebook has been created to accompany the *Grammar Tales* storybooks, a collection of beautifully illustrated books designed to support grammar and language development in children.

Including accessible activities and ideas to help children use grammar forms expressively, the guidebook discusses the specific grammatical form focused on in each story, and offers support in using the storybooks effectively. Photocopiable and downloadable handouts for parents and carers allow therapy work to continue beyond the therapy session.

This guidebook is an essential accompaniment to the *Grammar Tales* storybooks for speech and language therapists working with children.

Jessica Habib studied Speech Pathology at the University of Sydney, graduating in 2012. She has since worked with children in indigenous health, community, private, not-for-profit and education settings in both Australia and the UK. Jessica loves the privilege she has of seeing children thrive as they are guided to build and strengthen their communication skills.

Carina Ward is an illustrator based in the Blue Mountains, Australia. She works with watercolour and ink to create beautiful, bright images and likes to add a touch of humour to her work. Carina loves the way pictures tell stories and open up imaginary worlds.

T0383396

What's in the pack?

Guidebook

Pete and Jem

A Trip to the Zoo

Anything You Can Do

The Birthday Party

Time for Adventure!

Let's Go Shopping

Hide-and-Seek

A Day at the Beach

Access your online resources

Grammar Tales is accompanied by a number of printable online materials designed to ensure this resource best supports your professional needs.

To access your online resources:

Go to www.routledge.com/cw/speechmark and click on the image of this book's front cover.

Click the 'Sign in or Request Access' button and follow the instructions.

Supporting Grammar and Language Development in Children

A Guidebook for the *Grammar Tales* Stories

Jessica Habib

Routledge
Taylor & Francis Group

LONDON AND NEW YORK

Cover image: Carina Ward

First published 2023
by Routledge
4 Park Square, Milton Park, Abingdon, Oxon OX14 4RN

and by Routledge
605 Third Avenue, New York, NY 10158

Routledge is an imprint of the Taylor & Francis Group, an informa business

© 2023 Jessica Habib

The right of Jessica Habib to be identified as author of this work has been asserted in accordance with sections 77 and 78 of the Copyright, Designs and Patents Act 1988.

British Library Cataloguing-in-Publication Data
A catalogue record for this book is available from the British Library

Library of Congress Cataloging-in-Publication Data
A catalog record for this book has been requested

ISBN: 978-1-032-27435-5 (pbk)
ISBN: 978-1-003-29275-3 (ebk)

DOI: 10.4324/9781003292753

Typeset in Calibri
by Apex CoVantage, LLC

Access the companion website: www.routledge.com/cw/speechmark

Contents

Acknowledgements

This project, having lain dormant in my mind for a few years, was properly begun to keep me sane during the first UK COVID-19 lockdown. It continued in that vein for my wonderful illustrator and even better friend, Carina, who finished off the illustrations for eight picture books whilst homeschooling and keeping a baby and pre-schooler entertained as Sydneysiders fought their COVID-19 battle. No mean feat! It's hard to believe this was your first time illustrating picture books – I'm so glad you said yes!

Thank you to Karen, Sue and Jacey at Melbourn Primary School for looking over the manuscript of this guidebook with the eyes of TAs. Your feedback was invaluable; and working with you all even more so. To my favourite mother-in-law, Jeanette, and my super-encouraging Dad, Steve, for your careful proofreading; to my dear friend, Phillippa, for sharing life and your years of picture-book reading experience; and to my editor at Speechmark, Jane, and her team, you've been so helpful and approachable throughout the whole process. I'm so thankful for each of you.

And finally, to my husband, Tom. Thank you for encouraging me to turn this idea into a reality. Thank you for loving me like Jesus loves us. And here's to being published first!

About Grammar Tales

As a new speech pathologist working with young children in a community setting, I often came across clients who were experiencing difficulties with syntax and morphology; and I often felt out of my depth. I wasn't explicitly taught grammar until I went to university and would routinely need to go back to my books to feel confident to plan goals for these clients. This resource was as much born out of a need to further develop my own skills as it was out of a desire to help simplify the task of targeting grammar goals for clinicians.

In my clinical experience, I have enjoyed using picture books that were relevant to the client's goals as a springboard for activities and other goals in the session. I love this thematic approach because it allows linking and reinforcement of client goals, provides opportunity for developing pre-literacy skills and makes planning for sessions easier.

The purpose of this resource is to have a series of picture books each of which uses a sentence structure and morphological form repetitively to provide models of language covering a range of possible language therapy goals. Each story has two primary goals: first, to increase length and type of utterances; and second, a specific morphological form.

The books are designed to be used by speech pathologists/therapists in therapy sessions as a starting point for targeting their client's language goals. Introducing the session with the appropriate story book allows the clinician to model the target forms for the client. Suggestions are given in this guidebook for ways to target the goal expressively.

The books could also be given to parents/carers to use at home to reinforce what has been taught in the therapy session. Handouts can be given to assist with implementing carry-over activities at home.

Although it is ideal for children with language difficulties to see a speech therapist, this is often not possible; whether due to funding, location, length of waiting lists or other barriers. This resource therefore includes a section especially designed for educators, as a supplement to boosting the language skills of children in the classroom. Again, it is recommended that the picture books be read first and then one of the activity ideas be adopted to enable the children to use the target form themselves. This would be best done in small groups or 1:1, and parent/carer handouts could again be used.

The work of Brown (1973) in typical language acquisition has been used as the basis for the goals targeted in the set. Brown's Stage II, approximately equating to the language development of a typical 2–2.5 year old, forms the framework for the goals identified for this set of picture books. These books are appropriate to use with children in preschool or early primary school with whom the relevant language goals are being targeted.

Additionally, a narrative form with a beginning, middle (including complication) and end has been chosen to provide models for basic narrative structures. Use of picture books as a format has the added benefit of providing the opportunity for development of pre-literacy skills, which will be elaborated on further in Section 2 of this guide.

We know from the literature that children with language delays are likely to have a low MLU (Mean Length of Utterance) for their age, reduced sentence complexity, and immature development of grammar forms (Paul, 2007). This can impact their ability to communicate orally and participate in other grammar and language-based tasks (Smith-Lock et al., 2013), as well as having broader communication, social and emotional consequences throughout childhood and into adulthood (Leonard, 2000).

There is growing evidence for the effectiveness of speech pathology intervention for grammar targets. Part of any intervention program will include providing models (examples) of the target form for the child (e.g. Smith-Lock et al., 2013; Connell & Addison-Stone, 1992; Fey et al., 1993). It is essential for the child to have clearly understood and heard the target form before they will produce it. This picture-book series provides multiple models of target forms, allowing the child to hear the grammar structure repeatedly before being asked to produce it. Modelling alone is not likely to provide effective intervention (Connell & Addison-Stone, 1992), but it is an essential starting point for therapy. Suggested activities for therapy and home practice are included. These can be used as tools by the clinician/teacher/parent to encourage the child to use the target form when talking.

Reading aloud with children in their early years has been shown to have positive impacts on language development (e.g. Klein & Kogan, 2013). Picture books have the potential to be highly engaging through the use of characters, plots and illustrations. As such, they provide an ideal platform for providing models for therapy. They are also a highly helpful resource for the parent who may struggle to understand what is being asked of them for home practice.

Drawing from my own clinical experience, I have also endeavoured to ensure that this tool will assist in providing evidence-based language therapy, with the added benefit of supporting pre-literacy development. I hope it is of use to therapists, educators, parents and carers alike.

Jessica

Pre-literacy skills

Reading with young children is greatly beneficial for developing their pre-literacy skills, which build a strong foundation for learning to read and for a love of literature. Pre-literacy skills include:

- Print awareness
- Letter knowledge
- Language skills
- Phonological awareness

As you read with children using the *Grammar Tales* picture books, and in any other context, you may like to keep the following tips and strategies in mind (a modified version of this can be found in the parent/carer handouts in Section 6):

- Reading picture books helps teach children to hold books the right way up and to turn pages. You can model this, and ask the child to take a turn holding the book and turning the pages. You can also hold the books the wrong way and wait for the child to notice, stimulating a response from them.
- Occasionally point to words on the page as you read them. This shows that spoken words are connected to text and that text moves from left to right.

Pre-Literacy Skills

- Give children some early letter knowledge by pointing to letters you see in the text, naming the letter and making its sound. For example, 'Look, that's an 's'. Your name starts with an 's'. 'sss' for Sophie. That's the sound a snake makes. Can you make a snakey sound?'
- Build vocabulary by talking about words that may be new to the child and discussing their meaning.
- Encourage the child to make semantic links to the story by asking about a time they experienced something that happened in the book.
- Engage and involve the child in the story by talking with them about the pictures. This could include commenting on something in the picture or asking developmentally appropriate questions.
- If there is a repeatable language pattern in the story, pause to give the child the chance to fill in the sentence. For example, when reading 'Time for Adventure!': after you've read the phrase 'It is mine' a few times, you could pause after 'It is…' and give the child the chance to finish the sentence.
- Encourage the child to use their imagination and prediction skills by asking them what they think will happen next in the story.
- You may sometimes like to use books as a springboard for targeting a phonological awareness skill. For example, point out how the rhyming words in 'Anything You Can Do' sound the same; or practice identifying the initial sound of each of the food items that the children find in the grocery store in 'Let's Go Shopping'.
- Use varied intonation in your voice to help engage the child.
- The act of reading stories together helps to grow relationships. This is helpful in a therapy context and for parent–child relationships. Make the most of this and be sure to engage with the child during the story time. Parents/carers may like to take the opportunity to have a cuddle with their child while reading.
- Giving parents/carers books to take home with them can encourage a culture of reading in the home.

Notes for Educators

Section 5 and parts of Section 6 of this guide are primarily aimed at speech therapists, so please don't feel overwhelmed by them! You may be using them under the direction of a speech therapist, or you may have a classroom full of children with low language levels, who would benefit from books and activities which help increase the length of their spoken sentences and which help them to use particular parts of grammar correctly. I would suggest that in a classroom setting, they would be best used in a small group format by teachers or teaching assistants/teacher's aides. They could also be used in a special education setting. The books are best used in the order listed below, unless you notice a particular difficulty that would be beneficial to focus on.

The table below outlines the uses/goals for each picture book. Further detail on the grammar forms can be found in Section 5 if they are of interest. Activity ideas can be found in Section 5. They are also listed in the parent handouts (Section 6) at the end of this guidebook.

Picture book	Goals
Pete and Jem	1. To use sentences containing subject and verb clause elements. For example, 'The bird (subject) is running (verb)'. 2. To use the present progressive verb/words containing '-ing'. For example, 'swimm**ing**' or 'leap**ing**'.
A Trip to the Zoo	1. To use sentences containing subject, verb and object clause elements. For example, 'The girl (subject) cuddled (verb) the dogs (object)'. 2. To use regular plurals '-s'. For example, 'dog**s**'.
Anything You Can Do	1. To use sentences containing subject and verb clause elements. For example, 'I (subject) can run (verb)'. 2. To use pronouns 'I' and 'you'. 3. To use 'helping' (auxiliary) verbs 'can' and 'do'.
The Birthday Party	1. To use sentences containing subject and verb clause elements. For example, 'You (subject) are running (verb)'. 2. To use pronouns 'I' and 'you'. 3. To use helping verbs 'am', 'are' and 'is'.
Time for Adventure!	1. To use sentences containing subject, verb and object clause elements. For example, 'The ball (subject) is (verb) mine (object)'. 2. To use pronouns 'me', 'my', 'mine' and 'it'.

Picture book	Goals
Let's Go Shopping	1. To use sentences containing subject, verb and object clause elements. For example, 'The girl (subject) wanted (verb) a dog and cat (object)'. 2. To use the conjunction 'and' to list two items (not using 'and' to join two clauses). For example, 'I like apples **and** bananas.
Hide-and-Seek	1. To use sentences containing subject, verb and adverbial clause elements. For example, 'The girl (subject) looked (verb) under the dog (adverbial)'. 2. To use short phrases beginning with a preposition (prepositional phrases), such as '**under** the dog'. 3. To use prepositions including 'on', 'off', 'in', 'out' and 'under'.
A Day at the Beach	1. To use sentences containing subject, verb and object clause elements. For example, 'The girl (subject) cuddled (verb) the big dog (object)'. 2. To use early adjectives (big, small, little, long, quiet, loud, heavy, soft, fast, hot, cold, red, blue, yellow, green) to describe something.

Overview of grammar targets

Language is a key tool for communication. This resource is particularly focussed on assisting with the development of the rules (grammar) that structure language, specifically syntax and morphology. The rules of syntax govern the word order of sentences, while morphological rules determine how an individual word is organised (for instance, the word 'helped' contains two morphemes: the free morpheme 'help' and the bound morpheme '-ed').

Series 1 is aimed at children whose language development goals are in Brown's Stage II. Typically, children in this stage are aged 27–30 months; however, the child with a language disorder will be older when needing assistance to develop their grammatical forms. The mean length of utterance (MLU) for a child functioning in Brown's Stage II typically ranges from 2.0 to 2.5 morphemes per utterance (Brown, 1973). Sentences have therefore been kept short and restricted to Subject-Verb, Subject-Verb-Object and Subject-Verb-Adverbial clauses within a sentence. Sentences are of a simple clause type, in keeping with what is appropriate for these stages and with the goal of assisting the increase of sentence length and appropriate use of word order.

Each picture book aims to model a specific sentence structure (syntax) and a morphological form. These goals are listed in the 'Primary target/s' column. They are chosen because they are appropriate to target at this stage of language development. The target form is used repetitively to give the listener multiple models of how to use the particular component of grammar. Secondary targets are also used repetitively within most sentences but it is not an expectation that the child attempt to produce the secondary target. The secondary targets have been chosen to assist the formation of the sentence and because they are likely to be *understood* by a child in this stage of language acquisition.

Supporting Grammar and Language Development in Children

The table below details the clause, phrase and word types to be targeted in each book, as well as data for typical age of acquisition for the target forms.

Picture book	Clause type	Clause elements	Phrase elements	Word types	Example	Primary targets	Typical age of acquisition	Secondary target/s	Typical age of acquisition
Pete and Jem	Simple sentence	SUBJECT-VERB	Noun phrase Verb phrase	Noun/pronoun Auxiliary verb Present progressive verb.	Jem is jumping. They are crashing.	1. SV sentences 2. Present progressive verb (-ing)	1. 18–24 months 2. 19–28 months	A. Auxiliary verbs 'is and 'are' B. Pronoun 'they'	A. 30 months B. 35–40 months
A Trip to the Zoo	Simple sentence	SUBJECT-VERB-OBJECT	Noun phrase Verb phrase Noun phrase	Noun/pronoun (I, you, we) Present tense verb Regular plural	I like crocodiles. You like tigers. Belle likes snakes.	1. SVO sentences 2. Regular plural	1. 28–30 months 2. 27–30 months	A. Pronouns 'I', 'you', 'we'	A. 'I': 12–26 months 'You': 27–30 months 'We': 31–34 months
Anything You Can Do	Simple sentence	SUBJECT-VERB	Noun phrase Verb phrase	Pronouns (I, you) Auxiliary verb (can, do) Present tense verb	I can leap. You can crawl. Do you roar?	1. SV sentences 2. Pronouns (I, you) 3. Modal auxiliary verb 'can' 4. Auxiliary verb 'do'	1. 18–24 months 2. 'I': 12–26 months 'You': 27–30 months 3. 30 months 4. 27 months		

Overview of Grammar Targets

Picture book	Clause type	Clause elements	Phrase elements	Word types	Example	Primary targets	Typical age of acquisition	Secondary target/s	Typical age of acquisition
The Birthday Party	Simple sentence	SUBJECT-VERB	Noun phrase Verb phrase	Noun/pronouns (I, you) Auxiliary verb 'be' (am, are, is) Present progressive verb	I am wrapping. You are taping. Belle is sleeping.	1. SV sentence 2. Auxiliary verb 'be' (am, are, is) 3. Pronouns 'I' and 'you'.	1. 18–24 months 2. 30 months 3. 'I': 12–26 months 'You': 27–30 months	A. Present progressive verb	A. 19–28 months
Time for Adventure!	Simple sentence	SUBJECT-VERB-OBJECT	Noun phrase Verb phrase Noun phrase	Noun/ pronoun with possible article Verb/auxiliary verb (possible preposition 'to') Pronoun (me, it, my, mine)	It is mine. The puzzle belongs to me. It is my puzzle.	1. SVO sentences 2. Pronouns 'mine', 'me' 'my' and 'it'.	1. 28–30 months 2. 'mine', 'me' and 'my': 27–30 months; 'it': 12–26 months	A. Article 'the' B. Auxiliary 'is'	A. 35–40 months B. 30 months
Let's Go Shopping	Simple sentence	SUBJECT-VERB-OBJECT	Noun phrase Verb phrase Noun phrase	Pronoun Verb Noun Conjunction 'and' Noun	I find mangoes and papaya. You grab milk and cheese. We want lollies and popcorn.	1. SVO sentences 2. Conjunction 'and' (for listing)	1. 28–30 months 2. 25–27 months	A. Pronouns 'I', 'you', 'we'.	A. 'I': 12–26 months 'You': 27–30 months 'We': 31–34 months

Picture book	Clause type	Clause elements	Phrase elements	Word types	Example	Primary targets	Typical age of acquisition	Secondary target/s	Typical age of acquisition
Hide-and-Seek	Simple sentence	SUBJECT-VERB-ADVERBIAL	Noun phrase Verb phrase Prepositional phrase	Noun/pronoun 3rd person singular verb Prepositions (on, off, in, out, under) Article Noun	Pete hides under the table. Jem looks out the front.	1. SVA sentence 2. Prepositional phrases 3. Prepositions on, off, in, out, under	1. 24–30 months 2. By 36 months 3. on, in: 27–30 months; under: 12–24 months; off, out: 24–36 months	A. Articles B. 3rd person singular verb	A. 35–40 months B. 35–40 months
A Day at the Beach	Simple sentence	SUBJECT-VERB-OBJECT	Noun phrase Verb phrase Noun phrase	Noun/pronoun auxiliary 3rd person singular verb Adjective (big, small/little, long, loud, quiet, heavy, soft, fast, hot, cold, red, blue, yellow, green) Noun	Belle touches yellow sand.	1. SVO sentences 2. Adjectives (big, small/little, long, loud, quiet, heavy, soft, fast, hot, cold, red, blue, yellow, green)	1. 28–30 months 2. 24–36 months	A. Auxiliary 'is' B. 3rd person singular verb	A. 41–46 months B. 35–40 months

Grammar Tales picture books

This chapter includes activity ideas, along with a breakdown of the grammar for the text of the story, for each of the eight picture books in the series. The grammar has been broken down to a level of complexity deemed appropriate, and is not exhaustive. The activity ideas are designed to be used to teach the goal expressively <u>after</u> the target form has been modelled during reading. They can be used as part of a session with a speech therapist, in a classroom setting with a teacher or teaching assistant or at home with a parent/carer under the guidance of a speech therapist or educator (the handouts in Section 6 can be used to support home practice).

<u>Picture Book 1: Pete and Jem</u>

<u>Targets:</u> Subject-verb sentences with present progressive verbs.

<u>While reading the story:</u> Provide opportunities to produce the target form by asking, 'What is Jem doing?' There is a dog in each picture performing an action, giving further opportunities to encourage use of the present progressive verb.

<u>Activity ideas:</u>

- Look at the book again and ask the child to tell you what is happening on the page, prompting them to use the target form when necessary.
- Act out the actions that happen in the story. Ask: 'What are you doing?'

- Choose toys to act out the actions from the story. Ask: 'What is [toy] doing?'
- Play together with a play kitchen/doll's house/pirate ship/etc. and talk about what you/the doll/the pirate are/is doing. Ask: 'What are you/is your doll/is your pirate doing?'

A more detailed explanation of the sentence type used in this story can be seen in the table below:

Clause Type	Clause elements	Phrase elements	Main word types	Example	Primary targets	Typical age of acquisition	Secondary targets	Typical age of acquisition
Simple sentence	SUBJECT-VERB	Noun phrase Verb phrase	Proper noun Auxiliary verb Present progressive verb	Jem is jumping.	1. SV sentences 2. Present progressive verb (-ing)	1. 18–24 months 2. 19–28 months	A. Auxiliary verbs 'is' and 'are' B. Personal pronoun 'they'	A. 30 months B. 35–40 months

The text of the story along with a breakdown of the grammar is detailed below:

Page 2	Jem		is	patting.
Clause:	SUBJECT		VERB	
Phrase:	Noun phrase		Verb phrase	
Word:	Proper noun	Auxiliary verb	Present progressive verb	

Page 3	Pete	is	scratching.
Clause:	SUBJECT	VERB	
Phrase:	Noun phrase	Verb phrase	
Word:	Proper noun	Auxiliary verb	Present progressive verb
Page 4	Jem	is	giggling.
Clause:	SUBJECT	VERB	
Phrase:	Noun phrase	Verb phrase	
Word:	Proper noun	Auxiliary verb	Present progressive verb
Page 5	Pete	is	rolling.
Clause:	SUBJECT	VERB	
Phrase:	Noun phrase	Verb phrase	
Word:	Proper noun	Auxiliary verb	Present progressive verb
Page 6	Jem	is	throwing.
Clause:	SUBJECT	VERB	
Phrase:	Noun phrase	Verb phrase	
Word:	Proper noun	Auxiliary verb	Present progressive verb

Page 7	Pete	is	chasing.	
Clause:	SUBJECT		VERB	
Phrase:	Noun phrase		Verb phrase	
Word:	Proper noun	Auxiliary verb	Present progressive verb	
Page 8	Jem	is	jumping.	
Clause:	SUBJECT		VERB	
Phrase:	Noun phrase		Verb phrase	
Word:	Proper noun	Auxiliary verb	Present progressive verb	
Page 9	Pete	is	running.	
Clause:	SUBJECT		VERB	
Phrase:	Noun phrase		Verb phrase	
Word:	Proper noun	Auxiliary verb	Present progressive verb	
Page 10	They	are	crashing.	
Clause:	SUBJECT		VERB	
Phrase:	Noun phrase		Verb phrase	
Word:	Pronoun	Auxiliary verb	Present progressive verb	

Page 12	Jem	is	falling.	
Clause:	SUBJECT		VERB	
Phrase:	Noun phrase		Verb phrase	
Word:	Proper noun	Auxiliary verb	Present progressive verb	
Page 13	Pete	is	tumbling.	
Clause:	SUBJECT		VERB	
Phrase:	Noun phrase		Verb phrase	
Word:	Proper noun	Auxiliary verb	Present progressive verb	
Page 14	Jem	is	crying.	
Clause:	SUBJECT		VERB	
Phrase:	Noun phrase		Verb phrase	
Word:	Proper noun	Auxiliary verb	Present progressive verb	
Page 15	Pete	is	aching.	
Clause:	SUBJECT		VERB	
Phrase:	Noun phrase		Verb phrase	
Word:	Proper noun	Auxiliary verb	Present progressive verb	

Page 16	Mummy	is	cuddling.	
Clause:	SUBJECT		VERB	
Phrase:	Noun phrase		Verb phrase	
Word:	Proper noun		Auxiliary verb	Present progressive verb
Page 17	Daddy	is	kissing.	
Clause:	SUBJECT		VERB	
Phrase:	Noun phrase		Verb phrase	
Word:	Proper noun		Auxiliary verb	Present progressive verb
Page 18	Jem	is	standing.	
Clause:	SUBJECT		VERB	
Phrase:	Noun phrase		Verb phrase	
Word:	Proper noun		Auxiliary verb	Present progressive verb
Page 19	Pete	is	smiling.	
Clause:	SUBJECT		VERB	
Phrase:	Noun phrase		Verb phrase	
Word:	Proper noun		Auxiliary verb	Present progressive verb

Page 20	They	are	playing.
Clause:	SUBJECT	VERB	
Phrase:	Noun phrase	Verb phrase	
Word:	Pronoun	Auxiliary verb	Present progressive verb

Picture Book 2: A Trip to the Zoo

<u>Targets:</u> Subject-verb-object sentences with regular plurals

<u>While reading the story:</u> Emphasise the 's' at the end of each animal word.

<u>Activity ideas:</u>

- Look at the pictures in the book and encourage the child to count the number of animals on each page and then tell you how many there are using the plural form (e.g. 'there are two panda**s**'). And look out for some extra chameleons blending into their surroundings!
- Think together of other animals you might see at the zoo to help expand vocabulary. Draw pictures of these animals or make them from playdough and count how many you have, using the plural form (e.g. 'three wombat**s**').
- Talk about what animals you would see at a farm. Print and cut out pictures of farm animals and glue them onto a piece of paper with boxes to represent fences. Count the animals and encourage use of the plural form.
- Play with toy animals and talk about what the animals are doing. Make sure you have more than one of each animal so that it's easy to encourage use of plurals.

A more detailed explanation of the sentence type used in this story can be seen in the table below:

Clause Type	Clause elements	Phrase elements	Word types	Example	Primary targets	Typical age of acquisition	Secondary targets	Typical age of acquisition
Simple sentence	SUBJECT-VERB-OBJECT	Noun phrase Verb phrase Noun phrase	Noun/pronoun (I, you, we) Present tense verb Regular plural	I like crocodiles. You like seals. Belle likes chameleons.	1. SVO sentence. 2. Regular plural	1. 28–30 months 2. 27–30 months	A. Pronouns 'I', 'you', 'we'.	A. 'I': 12–26 months 'You': 27–30 months 'We': 31–34 months

The text of the story along with a breakdown of the grammar is detailed below:

Page 1	We	love	the	zoo!
Clause:	SUBJECT	VERB	OBJECT	
Phrase:	Noun phrase	Verb phrase	Noun phrase	
Word:	Pronoun	Present tense verb	Definite article	Noun
Page 2	We	like	elephants.	
Clause:	SUBJECT	VERB	OBJECT	
Phrase:	Noun phrase	Verb phrase	Noun phrase	
Word:	Pronoun	Present tense verb	Regular plural	

Page 4	We	like	giraffes.
Clause:	SUBJECT	VERB	OBJECT
Phrase:	Noun phrase	Verb phrase	Noun phrase
Word:	Pronoun	Present tense verb	Regular plural
Page 6	We.	like	monkeys
Clause:	SUBJECT	VERB	OBJECT
Phrase:	Noun phrase	Verb phrase	Noun phrase
Word:	Pronoun	Present tense verb	Regular plural
Page 7	Monkeys	love	bananas!
Clause:	SUBJECT	VERB	OBJECT
Phrase:	Noun phrase	Verb phrase	Noun phrase
Word:	Regular plural	Present tense verb	Regular plural
Page 8	Belle	likes	chameleons.
Clause:	SUBJECT	VERB	OBJECT
Phrase:	Noun phrase	Verb phrase	Noun phrase
Word:	Proper noun	3rd person singular verb	Regular plural

Page 9	Chameleons	like	hiding.
Clause: Phrase: Word:	SUBJECT Noun phrase Regular plural	VERB Verb phrase Present tense verb	OBJECT Noun phrase Gerund
Page 10	You	like	seals.
Clause: Phrase: Word:	SUBJECT Noun phrase Pronoun	VERB Verb phrase Present tense verb	OBJECT Noun phrase Regular plural
Page 11	I	like	crocodiles.
Clause: Phrase: Word:	SUBJECT Noun phrase Pronoun	VERB Verb phrase Present tense verb	OBJECT Noun phrase Regular plural
Page 12	Belle	wants	biscuits.
Clause: Phrase: Word:	SUBJECT Noun phrase Proper noun	VERB Verb phrase 3rd person singular verb	OBJECT Noun phrase Regular plural

Page 13	I	like	koalas.
Clause: Phrase: Word:	SUBJECT Noun phrase Pronoun	VERB Verb phrase Present tense verb	OBJECT Noun phrase Regular plural
Page 14	You	like	pandas.
Clause: Phrase: Word:	SUBJECT Noun phrase Pronoun	VERB Verb phrase Present tense verb	OBJECT Noun phrase Regular plural
Page 15	Belle	wants	toys.
Clause: Phrase: Word:	SUBJECT Noun phrase Proper noun	VERB Verb phrase 3rd person singular verb	OBJECT Noun phrase Regular plural
Page 16	I	like	meerkats.
Clause: Phrase: Word:	SUBJECT Noun phrase Pronoun	VERB Verb phrase Present tense verb	OBJECT Noun phrase Regular plural

Page 17	You	like	parrots.	
Clause: Phrase: Word:	SUBJECT Noun phrase Pronoun	VERB Verb phrase Present tense verb	OBJECT Noun phrase Regular plural	
Page 19	Parrots	like	ears.	
Clause: Phrase: Word:	SUBJECT Noun phrase Regular plural	VERB Verb phrase Present tense verb	OBJECT Noun phrase Regular plural	
Page 20	We	eat	chips.	
Clause: Phrase: Word:	SUBJECT Noun phrase Pronoun	VERB Verb phrase Present tense verb	OBJECT Noun phrase Regular plural	
Page 21	Mum	has	a	rest.
Clause: Phrase: Word:	SUBJECT Noun phrase Proper Noun	VERB Verb phrase Auxiliary verb	Indefinite article	OBJECT Noun phrase Noun

<u>Picture Book 3: Anything You Can Do</u>

<u>Targets:</u> Subject-verb sentences, singular personal pronouns (I, you), modal auxiliary verb (can) and auxiliary verb (do)

<u>While reading the story:</u> Ask questions as you read such as 'do you think the baby can swim?'

<u>Activity ideas:</u>

- If the child has siblings, talk about what things they can/can't do and what the sibling can/can't do. If they don't have siblings talk about what they think they can do that a baby can't do (e.g. 'I **can** hop'; 'Babies **can** smile').
- Do some actions together and ask each other '**can you** [action]?' with the response '**I can do** that'.
- Then try asking 'what **can I do**?' before doing an action, with the response '**You can** [action]'.
- Talk about likes and dislikes using the script: '**I like** ___. **Do you** like____?' Encourage full sentence responses, '**I like/don't like** ____.'

A more detailed explanation of the sentence type used in this story can be seen in the table below:

Clause Type	Clause elements	Phrase elements	Word types	Example	Primary targets	Typical age of acquisition	Secondary targets	Typical age of acquisition
Simple sentence	SUBJECT-VERB	Noun phrase Verb phrase Auxiliary verb (can, do) Present tense verb	Pronouns (I, you) Auxiliary verb (can, do) Present tense verb	I can leap. You can crawl. Do you roar?	1. SV sentences 2. Pronouns (I, you) 3. Modal auxiliary verb 'can' 4. Auxiliary verb 'do'	1. 18–24 months 2. 'I': 12–26 months 'You': 27–30 months 3. 30 months 4. 27 months	None	None

The text of the story along with a breakdown of the grammar is detailed below:

Page 2	You	can	leap.
Clause:	SUBJECT	VERB	
Phrase:	Noun phrase	Verb phrase	
Word:	Pronoun	Modal auxiliary verb	Present tense verb
Page 3	I	can	stumble.
Clause:	SUBJECT	VERB	
Phrase:	Noun phrase	Verb phrase	
Word:	Pronoun	Modal auxiliary verb	Present tense verb
Page 4	You	can	shoot.
Clause:	SUBJECT	VERB	
Phrase:	Noun phrase	Verb phrase	
Word:	Pronoun	Modal auxiliary verb	Present tense verb
Page 5	I	can	fumble.
Clause:	SUBJECT	VERB	
Phrase:	Noun phrase	Verb phrase	
Word:	Pronoun	Modal auxiliary verb	Present tense verb

Page 6	You	can	sprint.
Clause:	SUBJECT	VERB	
Phrase:	Noun phrase	Verb phrase	
Word:	Pronoun	Modal auxiliary verb	Present tense verb
Page 7	I	can	crawl.
Clause:	SUBJECT	VERB	
Phrase:	Noun phrase	Verb phrase	
Word:	Pronoun	Modal auxiliary verb	Present tense verb
Page 8	You	can	climb.
Clause:	SUBJECT	VERB	
Phrase:	Noun phrase	Verb phrase	
Word:	Pronoun	Modal auxiliary verb	Present tense verb
Page 9	I	can	fall.
Clause:	SUBJECT	VERB	
Phrase:	Noun phrase	Verb phrase	
Word:	Pronoun	Modal auxiliary verb	Present tense verb

Page 10	You	can	swim.
Clause: Phrase: Word:	SUBJECT Noun phrase Pronoun	VERB Verb phrase Modal auxiliary verb	 Present tense verb
Page 11	I	can	sink.
Clause: Phrase: Word:	SUBJECT Noun phrase Pronoun	VERB Verb phrase Modal auxiliary verb	 Present tense verb
Page 12	You	can	read.
Clause: Phrase: Word:	SUBJECT Noun phrase Pronoun	VERB Verb phrase Modal auxiliary verb	 Present tense verb
Page 13	I	can	think.
Clause: Phrase: Word:	SUBJECT Noun phrase Pronoun	VERB Verb phrase Modal auxiliary verb	 Present tense verb

Page 16	Do	you	tickle?	
Clause:	VERB	SUBJECT	(VERB)	
Phrase:	Verb phrase	Noun phrase	Verb phrase	
Word:	Auxiliary verb	Pronoun	Present tense verb	
Page 16	I	can	giggle!	
Clause:	SUBJECT	VERB		
Phrase:	Noun phrase	Verb phrase		
Word:	Pronoun	Modal auxiliary verb	Present tense verb	
Page 17	Do	you	jive?	
Clause:	VERB	SUBJECT	(VERB)	
Phrase:	Verb phrase	Noun phrase	Verb phrase	
Word:	Auxiliary verb	Pronoun	Present tense verb	
Page 17	I	can	jiggle!	
Clause:	SUBJECT	VERB		
Phrase:	Noun phrase	Verb phrase		
Word:	Pronoun	Modal auxiliary verb	Present tense verb	

Page 18	Do	you	roar?	
Clause:	VERB	SUBJECT	(VERB)	
Phrase:	Verb phrase	Noun phrase	Verb phrase	
Word:	Auxiliary verb	Pronoun	Present tense verb	
Page 18	I	can	hiss!	
Clause:	SUBJECT		VERB	
Phrase:	Noun phrase		Verb phrase	
Word:	Pronoun	Modal auxiliary verb	Present tense verb	
Page 19	Do	you	cuddle?	
Clause:	VERB	SUBJECT	(VERB)	
Phrase:	Verb phrase	Noun phrase	Verb phrase	
Word:	Auxiliary verb	Pronoun	Present tense verb	
Page 20	I	can	kiss!	
Clause:	SUBJECT		VERB	
Phrase:	Noun phrase		Verb phrase	
Word:	Pronoun	Modal auxiliary verb	Present tense verb	

Picture Book 4: The Birthday Party

Targets: Subject-verb sentences, present tense forms of the auxiliary verb 'to be' (am, is, are), singular personal pronouns (I, you)

While reading: Use gestures which show the actions in the story to support understanding of verbs, such as a mixing motion when you say 'mixing'.

Activity ideas:

- After reading, look at the pictures and talk about what the people are doing, e.g. 'What is Pete doing?' 'Pete is wrapping'.
- Do an activity together that allows you to talk about what you and the child are doing and about an object. For example, use playdough to prompt use of the primary targets: 'I **am** squishing', 'You **are** rolling'. Make your playdough creations perform actions you can talk about, e.g. 'The frog **is** jumping'.
- Ask the child to perform an action (e.g. 'jump') and then ask, 'What are you doing?', prompting a response of 'I **am** jumping'.
- Tell the child you are going to perform an action and that you want them to tell you what you are doing ('You **are** jumping').
- Play with toy cars together and talk about what they are doing e.g. 'The car **is** racing'.

A more detailed explanation of the sentence type used in this story can be seen in the table below:

Clause Type	Clause elements	Phrase elements	Word types	Example	Primary targets	Typical age of acquisition	Secondary targets	Typical age of acquisition
Simple sentence	SUBJECT-VERB	Noun phrase Verb phrase	Noun/Pronouns (I, you) Auxiliary verb 'be' (am, are, is) Present progressive verb	I am wrapping. You are taping. Belle is sleeping.	1. SV sentence 2. Auxiliary verb 'be' (am, are, is) 3. Pronouns 'I' and 'you'	1. 18–24 months 2. 30 months 3. 'I': 12–26 months 'You': 27–30 months	A. Present progressive verb	A. 19–28 months

The text of the story along with a breakdown of the grammar is detailed below:

Page 2	I	am	wrapping.	
Clause:	SUBJECT		VERB	
Phrase:	Noun phrase		Verb phrase	
Word:	Pronoun	Auxiliary verb	Present progressive verb	
Page 2	You	are	taping.	
Clause:	SUBJECT		VERB	
Phrase:	Noun phrase		Verb phrase	
Word:	Pronoun	Auxiliary verb	Present progressive verb	

Page 3	Belle		is		sleeping.		
Clause:	SUBJECT			VERB			
Phrase:	Noun phrase			Verb phrase			
Word:	Proper Noun		Auxiliary verb	Present progressive verb			
Page 4	I		am		mixing.		
Clause:	SUBJECT		VERB				
Phrase:	Noun phrase		Verb phrase				
Word:	Pronoun		Auxiliary verb	Present progressive verb			
Page 4	You		are		pouring.		
Clause:	SUBJECT		VERB				
Phrase:	Noun phrase		Verb phrase				
Word:	Pronoun		Auxiliary verb	Present progressive verb			
Page 5	The	cake		is		baking.	
Clause:	SUBJECT			VERB			
Phrase:	Noun phrase			Verb phrase			
Word:	Definite article	Noun		Auxiliary verb	Present progressive verb		

Page 6	I		am		licking.	
Clause:	SUBJECT		VERB			
Phrase:	Noun phrase		Verb phrase			
Word:	Pronoun		Auxiliary verb	Present progressive verb		
Page 6	You		are		icing.	
Clause:	SUBJECT		VERB			
Phrase:	Noun phrase		Verb phrase			
Word:	Pronoun		Auxiliary verb	Present progressive verb		
Page 7	It		is		ready!	
Clause:	SUBJECT		VERB		COMPLEMENT	
Phrase:	Noun phrase		Verb phrase		Adjectival phrase	
Word:	Pronoun		Auxiliary verb		Adjective	
Page 8	I		am		blowing.	
Clause:	SUBJECT		VERB			
Phrase:	Noun phrase		Verb phrase			
Word:	Pronoun		Auxiliary verb	Present progressive verb		

Page 9	You		are		blowing.	
Clause:	SUBJECT		VERB			
Phrase:	Noun phrase		Verb phrase			
Word:	Pronoun		Auxiliary verb	Present progressive verb		
Pages 10–13	[The balloon is ...] The	balloon		is...		whizzing!
Clause:	SUBJECT			VERB		
Phrase:	Noun phrase			Verb phrase		
Word:	Definite article	Noun		Auxiliary verb	Present progressive verb	
Page 14	I		am		waiting.	
Clause:	SUBJECT		VERB			
Phrase:	Noun phrase		Verb phrase			
Word:	Pronoun		Auxiliary verb	Present progressive verb		
Page 14	You		are		waiting.	
Clause:	SUBJECT		VERB			
Phrase:	Noun phrase		Verb phrase			
Word:	Pronoun		Auxiliary verb	Present progressive verb		

Page 15	Belle	is	waking.
Clause:	SUBJECT	VERB	
Phrase:	Noun phrase	Verb phrase	
Word:	Proper Noun	Auxiliary verb	Present progressive verb

Page 16	I	am	giving.
Clause:	SUBJECT	VERB	
Phrase:	Noun phrase	Verb phrase	
Word:	Pronoun	Auxiliary verb	Present progressive verb

Page 17	We	are	singing.
Clause:	SUBJECT	VERB	
Phrase:	Noun phrase	Verb phrase	
Word:	Pronoun	Auxiliary verb	Present progressive verb

Page 18	Belle	is	blowing.
Clause:	SUBJECT	VERB	
Phrase:	Noun phrase	Verb phrase	
Word:	Proper Noun	Auxiliary verb	Present progressive verb

Page 19	We		are	eating.	
Clause:	SUBJECT		VERB		
Phrase:	Noun phrase		Verb phrase		
Word:	Pronoun	Auxiliary verb	Present progressive verb		
Page 20	Happy	Birthday	Belle!		
Clause:	MINOR CLAUSE				
Phrase:					
Word:	Adjective	Noun	Proper noun		

Picture Book 5: Time for Adventure!

<u>Targets:</u> Subject-verb-object sentences, possessive and personal pronouns (mine, me, my, it)

<u>While reading:</u> Talk about how it is good to share things that belong to us with our friends. Talk about how you feel when someone doesn't share with you. Talk about how you feel when you take turns.

<u>Activity ideas:</u>

- Give a collection of toys or pictures to the child and keep a collection for yourself. Ask 'who has the [toy]' and model the response 'I have the [toy]. **It** is **mine**.' Prompt child to follow model when it is their turn. Depending on the child's goals, this activity could be performed using the response 'I have the [toy]. **It** belongs to **me**' or '**It** is **my** ball'.
- Notice items that belong to the child around the room. Ask 'whose (e.g.) hat is this?' Encourage the response '**It** is **mine**'/ '**It** belongs to **me**'/ '**It** is **my** hat'.
- Create a role play about sharing with dolls/toy figurines/toy animals. Each choose a toy to speak for and have one of the toys say, 'that is **mine**'/'that belongs to **me**'/'that is **my** ___'. Practise asking for toys and sharing.
- Have the child draw a picture of their family, while you draw a picture of your family. Model sentences containing the target words, e.g. 'This is **my** sister', 'This is **me**', 'that hat is **mine**'. Ask questions to help encourage the child to use the target words, e.g. 'Who is that?', 'Who does the dog belong to?'

A more detailed explanation of the sentence type used in this story can be seen in the table below:

Clause Type	Clause elements	Phrase elements	Word types	Example	Primary targets	Typical age of acquisition	Secondary targets	Typical age of acquisition
Simple sentence	SUBJECT-VERB-OBJECT	Noun phrase Verb phrase Noun phrase	Noun/pronoun with possible article Verb/auxiliary verb (possible preposition 'to') Pronoun (me, it, my, mine)	It is mine. The puzzle belongs to me. It is my puzzle.	1. SVO sentence 2. Pronouns 'mine', 'me' and 'my' and 'it'	1. 28–30 months 2. 'mine', 'me' and 'my': 27–30 months 'it': 12–26 months	A. Article 'the' B. Auxiliary 'is'	A. 35–40 months B. 30 months

The text of the story along with a breakdown of the grammar is detailed below:

Page 2	I	love	adventures!			
Clause:	SUBJECT	VERB	OBJECT			
Phrase:	Noun phrase	Verb phrase	Noun phrase			
Word:	Pronoun	Present tense verb	Regular plural			
Page 2	I	'm going	to	the	jungle.	
Clause:	SUBJECT	VERB	ADVERBIAL			
Phrase:	Noun phrase	Verb phrase	Prepositional phrase			
Word:	Pronoun	Auxiliary verb	Present progressive verb	Preposition	Article	Noun

Page 2	I	need		my	monkey.
Clause:	SUBJECT	VERB		OBJECT	
Phrase:	Noun phrase	Verb phrase		Noun phrase	
Word:	Pronoun	Present tense verb		Pronoun	Noun
Page 2	The monkey	belongs		to	me.
Clause:	SUBJECT	VERB		ADVERBIAL	
Phrase:	Noun phrase	Verb phrase		Prepositional phrase	
Word:	Article Noun	3rd person singular verb		Preposition	Pronoun
Page 2	It	is		mine!	
Clause:	SUBJECT	VERB		COMPLEMENT	
Phrase:	Noun phrase	Verb phrase		Noun phrase	
Word:	Pronoun	Auxiliary verb		Pronoun	
Page 4	I	smell		smoke!	
Clause:	SUBJECT	VERB		OBJECT	
Phrase:	Noun phrase	Verb phrase		Noun phrase	
Word:	Pronoun	Present tense verb		Noun	

Page 4	I		need		my	helmet.	
Clause:	SUBJECT		VERB		OBJECT		
Phrase:	Noun phrase		Verb phrase		Noun phrase		
Word:	Pronoun		Present tense verb		Pronoun	Noun	

Page 4	The	helmet	belongs		to	me.	
Clause:	SUBJECT		VERB		ADVERBIAL		
Phrase:	Noun phrase		Verb phrase		Prepositional phrase		
Word:	Article	Noun	3rd person singular verb		Preposition	Pronoun	

Page 4	It		is		mine!		
Clause:	SUBJECT		VERB		COMPLEMENT		
Phrase:	Noun phrase		Verb phrase		Noun phrase		
Word:	Pronoun		Auxiliary verb		Pronoun		

Page 6	I		hear	the	wicked	witch!	
Clause:	SUBJECT		VERB		OBJECT		
Phrase:	Noun phrase		Verb phrase		Noun phrase		
Word:	Pronoun		Present tense verb	Article	Adjective	Noun	

Page 6	I		need		my	magic	wand.
Clause:	SUBJECT		VERB		OBJECT		
Phrase:	Noun phrase		Verb phrase		Noun phrase		
Word:	Pronoun		Present tense verb		Pronoun	Adjective	Noun
Page 6	The	wand	belongs		to	me.	
Clause:	SUBJECT		VERB		ADVERBIAL		
Phrase:	Noun phrase		Verb phrase		Prepositional phrase		
Word:	Article	Noun	3rd person singular verb		Preposition	Pronoun	
Page 6	It		is		mine!		
Clause:	SUBJECT		VERB		COMPLEMENT		
Phrase:	Noun phrase		Verb phrase		Noun phrase		
Word:	Pronoun		Auxiliary verb		Pronoun		
Page 8	I		see		an	astronaut!	
Clause:	SUBJECT		VERB		OBJECT		
Phrase:	Noun phrase		Verb phrase		Noun phrase		
Word:	Pronoun		Present tense verb		Article	Noun	

Page 8	I			need		my	rocket	ship.	
Clause:	SUBJECT			VERB		OBJECT			
Phrase:	Noun phrase			Verb phrase		Noun phrase			
Word:	Pronoun			Present tense verb		Pronoun	Adjective	Noun	

Page 8	The	rocket		belongs			to	me.	
Clause:	SUBJECT			VERB			ADVERBIAL		
Phrase:	Noun phrase			Verb phrase			Prepositional phrase		
Word:	Article	Noun		3rd person singular verb			Preposition	Pronoun	

Page 8	It		is			mine!	
Clause:	SUBJECT		VERB		COMPLEMENT		
Phrase:	Noun phrase		Verb phrase		Noun phrase		
Word:	Pronoun		Auxiliary verb		Pronoun		

Page 12	Would		you	like	my	wand?	
Clause:	VERB		SUBJECT	(VERB)	OBJECT		
Phrase:	Verb phrase		Noun phrase	Verb phrase	Noun phrase		
Word:	Modal auxiliary verb		Pronoun	Present tense verb	Pronoun	Noun	

Page 12	You		can	fight		the	wicked	witch!
Clause:	SUBJECT		VERB			OBJECT		
Phrase:	Noun phrase		Verb phrase			Noun phrase		
Word:	Pronoun		Modal aux.	Present tense verb	Article	Adjective		Noun

Page 14	I		'll	keep		my	helmet.	
Clause:	SUBJECT		VERB			OBJECT		
Phrase:	Noun phrase		Verb phrase			Noun phrase		
Word:	Pronoun		Modal aux.	Present tense verb		Pronoun	Noun	

Page 14	I		can	rescue		you!		
Clause:	SUBJECT		VERB			OBJECT		
Phrase:	Noun phrase		Verb phrase			Noun phrase		
Word:	Pronoun		Modal aux.	Present tense verb		Pronoun		

Page 16	Would		you	like		my	monkey?	
Clause:	VERB		SUBJECT	(VERB)		OBJECT		
Phrase:	Verb phrase		Noun phrase	Verb phrase		Noun phrase		
Word:	Modal auxiliary verb		Pronoun	Present tense verb		Pronoun	Noun	

Page 16	He	will	swing	you	through	the	trees!
Clause:	SUBJECT	VERB		OBJECT	ADVERBIAL		
Phrase:	Noun phrase	Verb phrase		Noun phrase	Prepositional phrase		
Word:	Pronoun	Modal aux.	Present tense verb	Pronoun	Preposition	Article	Regular plural

Page 18	The	rocket	can	be	mine.
Clause:	SUBJECT		VERB		OBJECT
Phrase:	Noun phrase		Verb phrase		Noun phrase
Word:	Def. article	Noun	Modal aux.	Auxiliary verb	Pronoun

Page 18	It	will	fly	us	home!
Clause:	SUBJECT	VERB		OBJECT	ADVERBIAL
Phrase:	Noun phrase	Verb phrase		Noun phrase	Noun phrase
Word:	Pronoun	Modal aux.	Present tense verb	Pronoun	Noun

Page 20	I	love	going	on	adventures...
Clause:	SUBJECT	VERB		ADVERBIAL	
Phrase:	Noun phrase	Verb phrase		Prepositional phrase	
Word:	Pronoun	Present tense verb	Present progressive verb	Preposition	Regular Plural

Cont.	especially		with	my	friend!	
Clause:	ADVERBIAL		ADVERBIAL			
Phrase:	Adverbial Phrase		Prepositional phrase			
Word:	Adverb		Preposition	Pronoun	Noun	

Picture book 6: Let's Go Shopping

<u>Targets:</u> Subject-verb-object sentences, conjunction 'and' (for listing)

<u>While reading</u>: Emphasise the word 'and'.

<u>Activity ideas:</u>

- After reading the story together, look through the book again and ask the child what the characters found on each page. Encourage them to respond using 'and', e.g. 'she found apricots **and** cherries'. Also ask them to list other items they see on the page.
- Pretend to go shopping with toy food and baskets. Talk about what you are buying from the shops, e.g. 'I bought beans **and** spinach'. If you don't have toy food you could print and cut pictures of food and then glue them onto a picture of a shopping trolley.
- Talk about things you do/don't like and list them using '**and**'. This could be foods as well as other categories, e.g. sports, toys, colours, animals, etc.
- Talk about what you would need to make a cake. (e.g. 'We need flour **and** butter'.) Then show pictures of how to make a cake and talk about the procedure. Ask the child to retell the procedure using the pictures. Encourage use of '**and**', e.g. 'Add sugar **and** cocoa'. You could even make a cake together!

A more detailed explanation of the sentence type used in this story can be seen in the table below:

Clause Type	Clause elements	Phrase elements	Word types	Example	Primary targets	Typical age of acquisition	Secondary targets	Typical age of acquisition
Simple sentence	SUBJECT-VERB-OBJECT	Noun phrase Verb phrase Noun phrase	Pronoun Verb Noun Conjunction 'and' Noun	I find mangoes and papaya. You grab milk and cheese. We want lollies and popcorn.	1. SVO sentences 2. Conjunction 'and' (for listing)	1. 28–30 months 2. 25–27 months	A. Pronouns 'I', 'you', 'we'.	A. 'I': 12–26 months 'You': 27–30 months 'We': 31–34 months

The text of the story along with a breakdown of the grammar is detailed below:

Page 1	We		are	going		shopping.		
Clause:	SUBJECT		VERB			ADVERBIAL		
Phrase:	Noun phrase		Verb phrase			Noun phrase		
Word:	Pronoun		Auxiliary	Present progressive		Gerund		
Page 1	We		are	helping		Mum	and	Dad.
Clause:	SUBJECT		VERB			OBJECT		
Phrase:	Noun phrase		Verb phrase			Noun phrase		
Word:	Pronoun		Auxiliary	Present progressive		Proper noun	Conjunction	Proper noun

Page 2	I	find	mangoes	and	papaya.
Clause:	SUBJECT	VERB	OBJECT		
Phrase:	Noun phrase	Verb phrase	Noun phrase		
Word:	Pronoun	Present tense verb	Regular plural	Conjunction	Regular plural

Page 3	You	spot	apricots	and	cherries.
Clause:	SUBJECT	VERB	OBJECT		
Phrase:	Noun phrase	Verb phrase	Noun phrase		
Word:	Pronoun	Present tense verb	Regular plural	Conjunction	Regular plural

Page 4	I	get	bread	and	porridge.
Clause:	SUBJECT	VERB	OBJECT		
Phrase:	Noun phrase	Verb phrase	Noun phrase		
Word:	Pronoun	Present tense verb	Noun	Conjunction	Noun

Page 5	You	grab	milk	and	cheese.
Clause:	SUBJECT	VERB	OBJECT		
Phrase:	Noun phrase	Verb phrase	Noun phrase		
Word:	Pronoun	Present tense verb	Noun	Conjunction	Noun

Page 6	I	find	flour	and	sugar.	
Clause:	SUBJECT	VERB	OBJECT			
Phrase:	Noun phrase	Verb phrase	Noun phrase			
Word:	Pronoun	Present tense verb	Noun	Conjunction	Noun	
Page 7	You	see	spaghetti	and	rice.	
Clause:	SUBJECT	VERB	OBJECT			
Phrase:	Noun phrase	Verb phrase	Noun phrase			
Word:	Pronoun	Present tense verb	Noun	Conjunction	Noun	
Page 8	I	get	toothpaste	and	shampoo.	
Clause:	SUBJECT	VERB	OBJECT			
Phrase:	Noun phrase	Verb phrase	Noun phrase			
Word:	Pronoun	Present tense verb	Noun	Conjunction	Noun	
Page 9	You	find	nappies	and	wipes.	
Clause:	SUBJECT	VERB	OBJECT			
Phrase:	Noun phrase	Verb phrase	Noun phrase			
Word:	Pronoun	Present tense verb	Regular plural	Conjunction	Regular plural	

Page 10	We	see	lollies	and	popcorn.
Clause:	SUBJECT	VERB	OBJECT		
Phrase:	Noun phrase	Verb phrase	Noun phrase		
Word:	Pronoun	Present tense verb	Regular plural	Conjunction	Noun
Page 11	We	like	lollies	and	popcorn.
Clause:	SUBJECT	VERB	OBJECT		
Phrase:	Noun phrase	Verb phrase	Noun phrase		
Word:	Pronoun	Present tense verb	Regular plural	Conjunction	Noun
Page 12	We	want	lollies	and	popcorn.
Clause:	SUBJECT	VERB	OBJECT		
Phrase:	Noun phrase	Verb phrase	Noun phrase		
Word:	Pronoun	Present tense verb	Regular plural	Conjunction	Noun
Page 14	Uh oh!				
Clause:	MINOR CLAUSE				
Phrase:	Interjection				
Word:					

Page 16	I		say		sorry			to	Mum		and		Dad.
Clause:	SUBJECT		VERB		ADVERBIAL			ADVERBIAL					
Phrase:	Noun phrase		Verb phrase		Adjectival phrase			Prepositional phrase					
Word:	Pronoun noun		Present tense verb		Adjective			Preposition	Proper noun		Conjunction		Proper

Page 16	You		say		sorry			to	Mum		and		Dad.
Clause:	SUBJECT		VERB		ADVERBIAL			ADVERBIAL					
Phrase:	Noun phrase		Verb phrase		Adjectival phrase			Prepositional phrase					
Word:	Pronoun		Present tense verb		Adjective			Preposition	Proper noun		Conjunction		Proper noun

Page 17	We		say		sorry			to	the	lady	and		man.
Clause:	SUBJECT		VERB		ADVERBIAL			ADVERBIAL					
Phrase:	Noun phrase		Verb phrase		Adjectival phrase			Prepositional phrase					
Word:	Pronoun		Present tense verb		Adjective			Preposition	Article	Noun	Conjunction		Noun

Page 18	We		do	not	get			lollies		or		popcorn!	
Clause:	SUBJECT		VERB					OBJECT					
Phrase:	Noun phrase		Verb phrase					Noun phrase					
Word:	Pronoun		Auxiliary	Negative	Present tense verb			Regular plural		Conjunction		Noun	

<u>Picture Book 7: Hide-and-Seek</u>

<u>Targets:</u> Subject-verb-adverbial sentences, prepositional phrases, prepositions (on, off, in, out, under)

<u>While reading:</u> Emphasise the preposition in each sentence. Point to where the characters are hiding or looking to aid comprehension.

<u>Activity ideas:</u>

- After reading the story, look at it again together and ask questions to encourage the use of prepositions and prepositional phrases. For example, 'Where is Jem looking?'; '**On** the bookshelf'. If this is easy, encourage the use of a longer sentence 'Jem is looking **on** the bookshelf'. There are extra opportunities to use prepositions on the last page of the story.
- Place a ball **on/off/in/out of/under** a box and ask the child 'Where is the ball?'
- Hide objects around the room and when each one is found, ask where it was hidden.
- Play hide-and-seek and talk about where each person hid. You could also ask the child to say out loud where they are looking (e.g. 'I'm looking **under** the sheets').

Grammar Tales Picture Books

A more detailed explanation of the sentence type used in this story can be seen in the table below:

Clause Type	Clause elements	Phrase elements	Word types	Example	Primary targets	Typical age of acquisition	Secondary targets	Typical age of acquisition
Simple sentence	SUBJECT-VERB-ADVERBIAL	Noun phrase Verb phrase Prepositional phrase	Noun/pronoun 3rd person singular verb Prepositions (on, off, in, out, under) Article Noun	Pete hides under the table. Jem looks out the front.	1. SVA sentence 2. Prepositional phrases 3. Prepositions on, off, in, out, under	1. 24–30 months 2. By 36 months 3. on, in: 27–30 months; under: 12–24 months; off, out: 24–36 months	A. Articles B. 3rd person singular verb	A. 35–40 months B. 35–40 months

The text of the story along with a breakdown of the grammar is detailed below:

Page 2	Jem	counts	to	ten.		
Clause:	SUBJECT	VERB	ADVERBIAL			
Phrase:	Noun phrase	Verb phrase	Prepositional phrase			
Word:	Proper noun	Third person singular	Preposition	Noun		
Page 3	Pete	hides	under	the	bed.	
Clause:	SUBJECT	VERB	ADVERBIAL			
Phrase:	Noun phrase	Verb phrase	Prepositional phrase			
Word:	Proper noun	Third person singular	Preposition	Article	Noun	

Page 4	Belle		hides		in	the	toybox.	
Clause:	SUBJECT		VERB		ADVERBIAL			
Phrase:	Noun phrase		Verb phrase		Prepositional phrase			
Word:	Proper noun		Third person singular		Preposition	Article	Noun	

Page 5	Jem		looks		out	the	front.	
Clause:	SUBJECT		VERB		ADVERBIAL			
Phrase:	Noun phrase		Verb phrase		Prepositional phrase			
Word:	Proper noun		Third person singular		Preposition	Article	Noun	

Page 5	She		looks		in	the	bath.	
Clause:	SUBJECT		VERB		ADVERBIAL			
Phrase:	Noun phrase		Verb phrase		Prepositional phrase			
Word:	Pronoun		Third person singular		Preposition	Article	Noun	

Page 5	She		looks		under	the	rug.	
Clause:	SUBJECT		VERB		ADVERBIAL			
Phrase:	Noun phrase		Verb phrase		Prepositional phrase			
Word:	Pronoun		Third person singular		Preposition	Article	Noun	

Page 6	She		looks		on	the	bookshelf.	
Clause:	SUBJECT		VERB		ADVERBIAL			
Phrase:	Noun phrase		Verb phrase		Prepositional phrase			
Word:	Pronoun		Third person singular		Preposition	Article	Noun	
Page 7	Jem		finds		Belle!			
Clause:	SUBJECT		VERB		OBJECT			
Phrase:	Noun phrase		Verb phrase		Noun phrase			
Word:	Proper noun		Third person singular		Noun			
Page 8	Jem	and	Belle		look		for	Pete.
Clause:	SUBJECT				VERB		ADVERBIAL	
Phrase:	Noun phrase				Verb phrase		Prepositional phrase	
Word:	Proper noun	Conjunction	Proper noun		Verb		Preposition	Noun
Page 9	Jem		looks		in	the	cupboard.	
Clause:	SUBJECT		VERB		ADVERBIAL			
Phrase:	Noun phrase		Verb phrase		Prepositional phrase			
Word:	Proper noun		Third person singular		Preposition	Article	Noun	

Page 9	Belle		crawls		out	of	the	cupboard.
Clause:	SUBJECT		VERB		ADVERBIAL			
Phrase:	Noun phrase		Verb phrase		Prepositional phrase			
Word:	Proper noun		Third person singular		Prep.	Prep.	Article	Noun
Page 10	Jem		looks		on	the	windowsill.	
Clause:	SUBJECT		VERB		ADVERBIAL			
Phrase:	Noun phrase		Verb phrase		Prepositional phrase			
Word:	Proper noun		Third person singular		Preposition	Article	Noun	
Page 10	Belle		looks		under	the	blanket.	
Clause:	SUBJECT		VERB		ADVERBIAL			
Phrase:	Noun phrase		Verb phrase		Prepositional phrase			
Word:	Proper noun		Third person singular		Preposition	Article	Noun	
Page 11	Belle		looks		on	the	bed.	
Clause:	SUBJECT		VERB		ADVERBIAL			
Phrase:	Noun phrase		Verb phrase		Prepositional phrase			
Word:	Proper noun		Third person singular		Preposition	Article	Noun	

Page 11	She		climbs		off	the	bed.		
Clause:	SUBJECT		VERB		ADVERBIAL				
Phrase:	Noun phrase		Verb phrase		Prepositional phrase				
Word:	Pronoun		Third person singular		Preposition	Article	Noun		
Page 12	Jem		checks		on	the	trampoline.		
Clause:	SUBJECT		VERB		ADVERBIAL				
Phrase:	Noun phrase		Verb phrase		Prepositional phrase				
Word:	Proper noun		Third person singular		Preposition	Article	Noun		
Page 12	Belle		bounces		off	the	trampoline.		
Clause:	SUBJECT		VERB		ADVERBIAL				
Phrase:	Noun phrase		Verb phrase		Prepositional phrase				
Word:	Proper noun		Third person singular		Preposition	Article	Noun		
Page 13	Where		is		Pete?				
Clause:	QUESTION		VERB		OBJECT				
Phrase:	Adverbial Phrase		Verb phrase		Noun phrase				
Word:	Adverb		Auxiliary		Proper noun				

Page 16	They	find	Pete	under	the	bed!
Clause: Phrase: Word:	SUBJECT Noun phrase Pronoun	VERB Verb phrase Present tense verb	OBJECT Noun phrase Proper noun	ADVERBIAL Prepositional phrase Preposition		Article Noun

Page 17	Pete	counts	to	ten.
Clause: Phrase: Word:	SUBJECT Noun phrase Proper noun	VERB Verb phrase Third person singular	ADVERBIAL Prepositional phrase Preposition Noun	

Page 18	Where	is	Jem?
Clause: Phrase: Word:	QUESTION Adverbial Phrase Adverb	VERB Verb phrase Auxiliary	OBJECT Noun phrase Proper noun

Page 19	Where	is	Belle?
Clause: Phrase: Word:	QUESTION Adverbial Phrase Adverb	VERB Verb phrase Auxiliary	OBJECT Noun phrase Proper noun

Picture Book 8: A Day at the Beach

Targets: Subject-verb-object sentences, early adjectives

While reading: Encourage the development of prediction skills by asking the child what they think will happen next at a few points in the story.

Activity ideas:

- Look at the pictures in the book and ask questions to elicit adjectives. E.g. 'How do you think the water feels?' Encourage full sentence responses, e.g. 'The water feels **cold**'.
- Pull objects out of a 'feely' bag and ask the child to describe them, e.g. 'This is a **heavy** ball'; 'This is a **pink** dinosaur'; 'This is a **cold**-water bottle'.
- Perform an action (e.g. jump, sing, run) in a **big/small/loud/quiet/fast** manner and ask the child to tell you *how* you performed the action ('You did a **big** jump').
- Pair opposites together and compare them to increase understanding of the concept. For instance, have a **big** and **small** spoon and ask the child to identify which is big and which is small, and to use a sentence to describe them. You could do something similar for **hot/cold** and **loud/quiet**.

A more detailed explanation of the sentence type used in this story can be seen in the table below:

Clause Type	Clause elements	Phrase elements	Word types	Example	Primary targets	Typical age of acquisition	Secondary targets	Typical age of acquisition
Simple sentence	SUBJECT-VERB-OBJECT	Noun phrase Verb phrase Noun phrase	Noun/pronoun Auxiliary 3rd person singular verb Adjective (big, small/little, long, loud, quiet, heavy, soft, fast, hot, cold, colours) Noun	Belle touches yellow sand.	1. SVO sentences. 2. Adjectives (big, small/little, long, loud, quiet, heavy, soft, fast, hot, cold, colours)	1. 2–3 years 2. 28–30 months	A. Auxiliary 'is' B. 3rd person singular verb	A. 41–46 months B. 35–40 months

The text of the story along with a breakdown of the grammar is detailed below:

Page 2	It	is		a	hot	day.
Clause:	SUBJECT	VERB		OBJECT		
Phrase:	Noun phrase	Verb phrase		Noun phrase		
Word:	Pronoun	Auxiliary verb	Article	Adjective	Noun	

Page 2	Belle	touches		yellow	sand.	
Clause:	SUBJECT	VERB		OBJECT		
Phrase:	Noun phrase	Verb phrase		Noun phrase		
Word:	Proper noun	3rd person singular verb		Adjective	Noun	
Page 3	Pete	finds		a	little	shell.
Clause:	SUBJECT	VERB		OBJECT		
Phrase:	Noun phrase	Verb phrase		Noun phrase		
Word:	Proper noun	3rd person singular verb		Article	Adjective	Noun
Page 4	Jem	builds		a	big	sandcastle.
Clause:	SUBJECT	VERB		OBJECT		
Phrase:	Noun phrase	Verb phrase		Noun phrase		
Word:	Proper noun	3rd person singular verb		Article	Adjective	Noun
Page 5	They	hear		quiet	waves.	
Clause:	SUBJECT	VERB		OBJECT		
Phrase:	Noun phrase	Verb phrase		Noun phrase		
Word:	Noun	Present tense verb		Adjective	Regular plural	

Page 6	Belle		sees			grey	sky.	
Clause:	SUBJECT		VERB		OBJECT			
Phrase:	Noun phrase		Verb phrase		Noun phrase			
Word:	Proper noun		3rd person singular verb			Adjective	Noun	

Page 7	Jem		has		a	red	bucket.	
Clause:	SUBJECT		VERB		OBJECT			
Phrase:	Noun phrase		Verb phrase		Noun phrase			
Word:	Proper noun		Auxiliary verb		Article	Adjective	Noun	

Page 7	She		sees		a	long	fish.	
Clause:	SUBJECT		VERB		OBJECT			
Phrase:	Noun phrase		Verb phrase		Noun phrase			
Word:	Pronoun		3rd person singular verb		Article	Adjective	Noun	

Page 8	Pete		sees		fast	crabs.		
Clause:	SUBJECT		VERB		OBJECT			
Phrase:	Noun phrase		Verb phrase		Noun phrase			
Word:	Proper noun		3rd person singular verb		Adjective	Regular plural		

Page 8	He	has	a	green	snorkel.		
Clause:	SUBJECT	VERB		OBJECT			
Phrase:	Noun phrase	Verb phrase		Noun phrase			
Word:	Pronoun	Auxiliary verb	Article	Adjective	Noun		
Page 9	They	feel	cold	water.			
Clause:	SUBJECT	VERB	OBJECT				
Phrase:	Noun phrase	Verb phrase	Noun phrase				
Word:	Pronoun	Verb	Adjective	Noun			
Page 10	Belle	hears	loud	thunder.			
Clause:	SUBJECT	VERB		OBJECT			
Phrase:	Noun phrase	Verb phrase		Noun phrase			
Word:	Proper noun	3rd person singular verb		Adjective	Noun		
Page 11	She	feels	heavy	rain.			
Clause:	SUBJECT	VERB		OBJECT			
Phrase:	Noun phrase	Verb phrase		Noun phrase			
Word:	Pronoun	3rd person singular verb	Adjective	Noun			

Page 14	They		watch		the	big	storm.		
Clause:	SUBJECT		VERB		OBJECT				
Phrase:	Noun phrase		Verb phrase		Noun phrase				
Word:	Pronoun		Verb		Article	Adjective	Noun		
Page 14	They		snuggle			in	soft	towels	
Clause:	SUBJECT		VERB		ADVERBIAL				
Phrase:	Noun phrase		Verb phrase		Prepositional phrase				
Word:	Pronoun		Verb		Preposition	Adjective	Noun		
Page 15	Dad		drives		the	fast	car.		
Clause:	SUBJECT		VERB		OBJECT				
Phrase:	Noun phrase		Verb phrase		Noun phrase				
Word:	Proper noun		3rd person singular verb		Article	Adjective	Noun		
Page 18	Pete		gets			his	green	snorkel.	
Clause:	SUBJECT		VERB		OBJECT				
Phrase:	Noun phrase		Verb phrase		Noun phrase				
Word:	Proper noun		3rd person singular verb		Pronoun	Adjective	Noun		

Page 18	Jem		gets		her	blue	snorkel.
Clause:	SUBJECT		VERB		OBJECT		
Phrase:	Noun phrase		Verb phrase		Noun phrase		
Word:	Proper noun		3rd person singular verb		Pronoun	Adjective	Noun
Page 18	Belle		gets		her	little	bucket.
Clause:	SUBJECT		VERB		OBJECT		
Phrase:	Noun phrase		Verb phrase		Noun phrase		
Word:	Proper noun		3rd person singular verb		Pronoun	Adjective	Noun
Page 19	They		have	a	loud	bath!	
Clause:	SUBJECT		VERB		OBJECT		
Phrase:	Noun phrase		Verb phrase		Noun phrase		
Word:	Pronoun		Auxiliary verb	Article	Adjective	Noun	

Handouts for parent/carers

The following pages contain handouts that can be photocopied and given to parents or carers to assist with reinforcing goals at home. Handouts are included on the following topics

- Reading with your child: pre-literacy skills
- Helping your child use longer sentences: developing language
- Learning to use '-ing' words: present progressive verb
- Learning to use plurals: regular plurals
- Learning to say 'can' and 'do': modal auxiliary verbs 'can' and 'do'
- Learning to say 'you', 'I' and 'it': singular personal pronouns
- Learning to say 'am', 'is' and 'are': present tense forms of the auxiliary verb 'to be'
- Learning to say 'me', 'mine' and 'my': personal & possessive pronouns
- Learning to say 'and' to list things: conjunction 'and' for listing
- Learning to say 'on', 'off', 'in', 'out', 'under': location prepositions and prepositional phrases
- Learning to use describing words: early adjectives

Reading with your child – Pre-literacy skills

One of the best things you can do to help prepare your child to read for themselves is to read *to* them. Reading picture books with your child helps them to learn about how books work and is great for increasing their vocabulary and knowledge of the world. Here are some ideas that will help your child get the most out of the time that you spend reading with them:

- Enjoy a cuddle with your child while you read to them.
- Reading picture books helps teach children to hold books the right way up and to turn pages. You can model this and ask the child to take a turn holding the book and turning the pages. You can also hold the books the wrong way and wait and see if your child notices.
- Occasionally point to words on the page as you read them. This shows that spoken words are connected to text and that text moves from left to right.
- Give your child some early letter knowledge by pointing to letters you see in the text, naming the letter, and making its sound. For example, 'Look, that's an 's'. Your name starts with an 's'. 'sss' for Sophie. That's the sound a snake makes. Can you make a snakey sound?'
- Talk about words that might be new to your child and discuss what they mean.
- Encourage your child to talk about a time they experienced something that happened in the book.

- Engage and involve your child in the story by talking with them about the pictures. You might talk about things you see in the picture or ask them questions that start with words like 'where', 'who' and 'what'.
- If there is a repeatable language pattern in the story, pause to give the child the chance to fill in the sentence. For example, when reading 'Time for Adventure', after you've read the phrase 'It is mine' a few times, you could pause after 'It is...' and give the child the chance to finish the sentence.
- Encourage the child to use their imagination and prediction skills by asking them what they think will happen next in the story.
- If there are words in the book that rhyme, point these out and think together of another rhyming word.
- Use an interesting voice to help keep your child's attention.
- Let your children see you reading and have things to read around the house. If you don't have many books you can always borrow some from the library for free!

Helping your child use longer sentences - Developing language

Learning language is foundational for communication, reading and preparing for school. Sometimes it can be tricky for children to learn new words and how to speak in sentences, so they may need a helping hand along the way. You can use the ideas below to help support the development of your child's language.

- Talk to your child LOTS! Talk about the things you see around you, what you are doing, where you are going …
- Name things you can see and point to them. This helps to increase your child's vocabulary.
- Pause and wait for your child to talk. Count to ten slowly in your head to help you wait.
- Play with your child. Get down to their level. Notice what they are interested in and talk about that.
- Make up imaginary worlds together and pretend their toys are talking to each other. If you show them how to do this they may soon catch on!
- Make eye contact with your child and use gestures to support your words.
- If your child says something, add to what they say, e.g. Child: 'Car!' Parent: 'Yes, a red car! Red car.' For children who use slightly longer sentences, you can show them how to lengthen their sentences even more, e.g. Child: 'Red car is driving!' Parent: 'Yes, the red car is driving fast!' or 'The red car is driving on the road'.

- If your child says something incorrectly, repeat it back to them correctly. E.g. Child: 'Mummy going shop' Parent: 'Hm ... Mummy is going to the shops, isn't she?' There's no need to ask your child to say it again or to tell them they said it wrong, just model the correct grammar for them.
- Read books together! Picture books expose children to new vocabulary and model good sentence structures.
- Keep use of devices to a minimum. Children learn language much more effectively from people than TV.
- Keep any instructions you give your child short to give them the best possible chance to understand. If they seem to understand your instructions easily, try giving them instructions with more steps (e.g. 'Please put your boots on and then get your coat').
- If your child isn't talking much, keep your sentences nice and short to help them to understand and learn new words.

Learning to use '-ing' words –
Present progressive verbs

- Read 'Pete and Jem' together. Look at the pictures and ask your child questions like 'what is Jem doing?' or 'what is Pete doing?' If they answer using an '-ing' word (e.g. 'running'), praise their good talking. If they don't use an '-ing' word, say 'can you try that again with 'runn**ing'?**'
- If you notice your child not saying an '-ing' word properly when they're talking, repeat the sentence back to them using correct grammar, e.g. if your child says 'he is run' you could respond 'yeah, he is runn**ing**'.
- Play a game in which you take turns giving each other a movement to do (e.g. run, jump, hop). While the person is doing their movement, they need to say, 'I am (e.g.) hopp**ing**'. They get a point if they say the sentence correctly.
- Have a picnic in the park and talk about what you can see people doing (e.g. 'He is kick**ing**', 'she is climb**ing'**).
- When you're playing with your child, ask what their toys are doing and talk about what your toys are doing (e.g. 'My bunny is sleep**ing**').

Learning to use plurals - Regular plurals

- Read 'A Trip to the Zoo' together. Make a nice loud 'sss' sound for plural words (e.g. 'panda**s**'). Ask your child to help you count the number of animals on each page. If he forgets to make the word a plural, remind him.
- If you notice your child not using plurals when she should in general conversation, repeat the sentence back to her using correct grammar, e.g. if your child says, 'there are lots of bird!' you could respond 'hm there are lots of bird**s** aren't there?'
- Play with toys at home that you have multiples of (e.g. two teddies, three dolls) and talk about what they are doing. Remind your child to add an 's' to the end if they forget.
- Talk about things you have at home and ask how many there are. For example, you could ask your child to help you set the table and ask them, 'How many fork**s** do we need?' and encourage the response, 'we need five fork**s**'. You could repeat this with spoons, knives, plates, cups, etc.
- Have your child help you put washing into piles of shirts/shorts/jumpers/etc as you fold washing. As you give them an item, ask them to tell you which pile it should go in. If needed, remind them to use a 's' to show that they are talking about more than one of something.

Learning to say 'can' and 'do' - Modal auxiliary verbs 'can' and 'do'

- Read 'Anything You Can Do' together. Talk together about what you can see the children in the pictures doing.
- Talk with your child about things that a younger child they know can or can't do. If you don't know any younger children personally, talk about what they think a baby could do, e.g. 'Babies **can** smile'.
- Do some actions (e.g. clap, spin, stretch, leap) together and ask each other '**can** you [action]?' with the response 'I **can do** that'.
- Then try asking 'what **can** I **do**?' before doing an action, with the response 'You **can** [action]'.
- Ask questions using the words 'can' and 'do' while you do an activity together. For instance, if you are drawing pictures together, you could ask '**Can** you draw a tiger?' or '**Do** you like my circle?' Encourage them to respond using a sentence, e.g. 'I **can** draw a tiger' or 'I **do** like your circle'.

Learning to say 'you', 'I' and 'it' – Singular personal pronouns

- Read 'Anything You Can Do' and/or 'The Birthday Party' together.
- Talk about likes and dislikes using the script: 'I like ____. Do you like____?' Encourage full sentence responses, 'I like/don't like ____.'
- Play with playdough together and talk about what you are doing using the target words. E.g. '**I** am squishing', '**you** are rolling'. Make your playdough creations perform actions you can talk about, e.g. '**it** is jumping'.
- Ask your child to perform an action (e.g. 'jump') and then ask, 'what are **you** doing?', prompting a response of '**I** am jumping'.
- Tell your child you are going to perform an action and that you want them to tell you what you are doing ('**You** are jumping').
- Play with toy cars together and talk about what one of the cars is doing e.g. '**it** is racing'.

Learning to say 'am', 'is' and 'are' – Present tense forms of the auxiliary verb 'to be'

- Read 'The Birthday Party' together. Say the target word/s ('am', 'is', 'are') slowly and clearly.
- After reading, look at the pictures and talk about what the people are doing, e.g. 'What is Pete doing?' 'Pete is wrapping'.
- Play with playdough together and talk about what you are doing using the target words. E.g. 'I **am** squishing', 'you **are** rolling'. Make your playdough creations perform actions you can talk about, e.g. 'it **is** jumping'.
- Ask the child to perform an action (e.g. 'jump') and then ask, 'what are you doing?', prompting a response of 'I **am** jumping'.
- Tell the child you are going to perform an action and that you want them to tell you what you are doing ('You **are** jumping').
- Play with toy cars together and talk about what they are doing e.g. 'it **is** racing'.
- Ask your child at different moments during the day 'what are you doing?', giving them the opportunity to respond 'I **am** _____' in a less structured context.

Learning to say 'me', 'mine' and 'my' –
Singular personal and possessive pronouns

- Read 'Time for Adventure!' together.
- Give your child a collection of things that belong to them in a bag, and keep a bag with a collection of things that belong to you. Ask 'who has the (e.g.) ball' and model the response 'I have the ball. It is **mine**.' Remind them to use the word 'mine' when it is their turn. Depending on your child's goals, this activity could be performed using the response 'I have the ball. It belongs to **me'** or 'It is **my** ball'.
- Notice items that belong to your child around the room. Ask 'whose (e.g.) hat is this?' Encourage the response 'It is **mine**'/ 'It belongs to **me**'/ 'It is **my** hat'.
- Ask about items at home while you're getting ready for the day. E.g. 'Whose drink bottle is this?'
- Create a role play about sharing with dolls/toy figurines/toy animals. Each choose a toy to speak for and have one of the toys say, 'that is **mine**'/ 'that belongs to **me**'/ 'it is **my** ___'. Practise asking for toys and sharing.

Learning to Say 'and' to list things –
Conjunction 'and' for listing

- Read 'Let's Go Shopping' with your child. Then look through the book again and ask your child what the characters found on each page. Encourage them to respond using 'and', e.g. 'she found apples **and** bananas'. Also ask them to list other items they see on the page.
- Pretend to go shopping with toy food and baskets. Talk about what you are buying from the shops, e.g. 'I bought beans **and** spinach'. If you don't have toy food you could print and cut pictures of food and then blutac them onto a picture of a shopping trolley.
- Talk about things you do/don't like and list them using **'and'**. This could be foods as well as other categories, e.g. sports, toys, colours, animals, etc.
- Make cupcakes together (use a packet mix to keep it simple!) and talk about what needs to go in the mixture as you go. Afterwards, ask your child to tell you what you did, e.g. 'What did we put into the bowl?' 'eggs **and** butter'.
- When getting ready for the day, ask your child to help you remember what you need to pack, e.g. 'We need water bottles **and** sandwiches'.

Learning to say 'on', 'off', 'in', 'out' and 'under' - Location prepositions and prepositional phrases

- Read 'Hide-and-Seek' together. After reading the story, look at it again and ask questions that start with 'where'. For example, 'Where is Jem looking?'; '**On** the roof', or 'Where is Pete hiding?'; '**Under** the table'. If this is easy for them, encourage the use of a longer sentence: 'Jem is looking **on** the roof'.
- Place a ball **on/off/in/out of/under** a box and ask your child 'Where is the ball?'
- Hide objects around the room and when each one is found, ask where it was hidden.
- Play-hide-and seek and talk about where each person hid. You could also ask your child to say out loud where they are looking (e.g. 'I'm looking **under** the sheets').
- Show how to use the target words during household tasks. For example, when hanging out the washing say '**on** the line' and when taking off the washing say '**off** the line'; or when putting an ingredient in a bowl for a salad say '**in** the bowl'; when taking toys out of a box say '**out** of the box'; when putting shoes away say '**under** the bed'. If you are looking to extend the length of your child's sentences, model the full sentence, e.g. 'I'm putting your shoes **under** the bed'. You can also encourage the child to use a sentence by asking, (e.g.) 'Where do your shoes go?'

Learning to use describing words -
Early adjectives

- Read 'A Day at the Beach' together. Look at the pictures as you read and ask questions to encourage your child to describe things in the story. E.g. 'How do you think the water feels?'; 'The water feels **cold**', or 'Tell me about the bucket'; 'The bucket is **red**'. As much as possible, encourage them to use full sentences rather than single word responses.
- Collect a bag of objects for your child to pull out and describe, e.g. 'This is a **heavy** ball'; 'This is a **pink** dinosaur'; 'This is a **cold** drink bottle'.
- Perform an action (e.g. jump, sing, run) in a **big/small/loud/quiet/fast** manner and ask your child to tell you *how* you performed the action. ('You did a **big** jump').
- Notice things in your daily activities that your child could describe: Is the bath water **hot** or **cold**? Are the cars driving past **loud** or **quiet**, **fast** or **slow**? What **colour** cars can you see? What **colour** crayons are you drawing with? Are the dogs walking past **big** or **small**?
- Go to a beach or park and talk about what you can see/hear/touch using describing words.

References

Ball, D. M. J., Crystal, D., & Fletcher, P. (Eds (2012). *Assessing grammar: The languages of LARSP* (Bristol: Channel View Publications).

Bowen, C. (1998). Brown's Stages of Syntactic and Morphological Development. Retrieved from www.speech-language-therapy.com/index.php?option=com_content&view=article&id=33 on 21/07/2020.

Brown, R. (1973). *A First Language: The Early Stages.* (Cambridge, MA. Harvard University Press).

Connell, P. & Addison-Stone, C. (1992). Morpheme learning of children with specific language impairment under controlled instructional conditions. *Journal of Speech, Language and Hearing Research*, 35, 844–852.

Fey, M. E., Cleave, P. L. & Long, S. H. (1993). Speech, Language approaches to the facilitation of grammar in children with language impairment. *Journal of Speech, Language and Hearing Research*, 36, 141–157.

Kidsense Child Development Corporation (2020). Stages of Language Development Chart. Retrieved from https://childdevelopment.com.au/resources/child-development-charts/stages-of-language-development-chart/ on 21/07/2020.

Klein, O. & Kogan, I. (2013). Does reading to children enhance their educational success? Short- and long-term effects of reading to children in early childhood on their language abilities, reading behavior and school marks. *Child Indicators Research*, 6, 321–344.

Lanza, J. R., & Flahive, L. K. (2008). *Linguisystems Guide to Communication Milestones* (East Moline, IL: LinguiSystems, Inc.)

Leonard, L. B. (2000). *Children with Specific Language Impairment* (Cambridge, MA: MIT Press).

Owens, Robert E. (2012). *Language Development: An Introduction*. 8th ed. Harlow: Pearson Education.

Paul, R. (2007). *Language Disorders from Infancy Through Adolescence: Assessment and Intervention.* 3rd Ed. (St Louis, Missouri: Mosby Elsevier).

Smith-Lock, K.M., Leitao, S., Lambert, L., & Nickels, L. (2013). Effective Intervention for expressive grammar in children with Specific Language Impairment. *International Journal of Language and Communication Disorders,* 48 (3), 265–282.